BEING COMPLEX WITHOUT HAVING A COMPLEX

Dr. Tony Picchioni, PhD

PublishAmerica
Baltimore

First printing

PublishAmerica has allowed this work to remain exactly as the author intended, verbatim, without editorial input.

Hardcover 978-1-4512-7498-1
Softcover 978-1-4512-7497-4
PUBLISHED BY PUBLISHAMERICA, LLLP
www.publishamerica.com
Baltimore

Printed in the United States of America

INTRODUCTION

This little book grew out of my experience in assisting people who wanted to work more effectively together on jobs, committees, or boards. In some cases, they struggled within marriage or some other close relationship in the hope of forestalling communications breakdown. My responsibility became that of helping to restore both mutual respect and effective lines of communication. For years, I worked also to assist the individual to communicate more effectively with himself or herself. The following chapters offer insights and techniques for strengthening cooperation rather than dominance, submission, or hostility.

The book addresses also methods for redirecting energy away from reactions that undermine and toward interactions that reinforce the mutual aid of creative relationships. Early on, human beings had to become creative in their bid for survival. After eventually developing tactics to stabilize basic survival, new interests and goals emerged. We not only survived, but also found ways to enjoy interest-filled lives. Since an interesting life ordinarily involves associating with other people, learning how to work and play well in groups became imperative.

Our ancestors had to learn teamwork when hunting food. In that respect, we are like another highly social animal, the wild dog, an amazing creature that survives by consistent cooperation. Our ancestors had the option of either assisting each other in the hunt or becoming themselves the prey. A human being alone in the wild with powerful carnivores is scarcely more than wild game. Together, however, human individuals bonded by astonishing acts of collaboration could bring down prey many times the size a single human mortal.

The philosopher Herbert Spencer came up with the catchy metaphor "survival of the fittest." What is often forgotten is Spencer's more important study of the pleasure felt in human sociality and in the countless rewards gained only through cooperative ventures. His writings in sociology, psychology, ethics, and even biology bring to light the necessity of mutual assistance. In fact, his psychology is a social psychology that has deep roots in cooperation at the biological level.

Human sympathy adds the *feeling tone* that both reflects and contributes to the overt fact of mutuality. Some researchers have suggested that the amoeba can react only if physically touched. We as human beings, by contrast, can be touched and profoundly moved by the plights and suffering of people we have never seen or heard. Astonishingly sensitive, we can be touched in countless ways. The following pages explore details of the 5 Rs, which are techniques for moving beyond dysfunctional relationships and toward cooperation, beyond breakdown and toward the reciprocal reinforcement that increases the chances of reaping the rewards of a dynamic harmony.

I will discuss the 5 Rs in this order:
1. Refract
2. Resurge
3. Reorganize
4. Rehearse
5. Resonate

They are not steps, however, but the major ingredients of the process of rerouting dysfunctional impulsiveness toward dynamic harmony on the personal and social levels. No one of the ingredients necessarily comes before the others. To refract anger or other impulses, we need to reorganize some of our thinking. But we can improve our thinking and actions by rehearsal. In other words, the 5 Rs interact continually as each enhances the others as in good cooking. It does not matter which one we focus on first. The important thing is to include them all and to develop a *feel* or *taste* for each one. Jut as we ingest nourishment to strengthen the body, so we can ingest and absorb the 5 Rs as nourishment for mind and heart. The goal is to resurge with self-awareness, self-control, and a better way of resonating with others.

As I cast the familiar sometimes in a different light or suggest other ways of looking at situations, I hope these jargon-free pages strike you as common sense. The goal is to offer clues for fine-tuning certain areas of relationships with family, friends, or fellow employees as well as employers. Elizabeth's family had seen the same painting in the family room for nine years. One day she pointed to a face in the trees beside the river and called attention to other "images" that were there all along, depending on the way the viewer perceived them. Thereafter, it became a different painting in many ways.

REFRACT

The Prism. As children we delighted in seeing a spectrum of colors appear on the wall as the sun shone through the window. Later, we learned that the prism in the window refracted the light by altering the course of wave energy. Our minds can function as prisms to catch our raw impulses and spread them out in an array of diversity. This allows us to see anger, for example, as not one simple "thing," but a spectrum of different emotions, thoughts, and suppositions. It follows that there is no one automatic response to another person's anger. Furthermore, we can learn to send our own anger through our mental prism. The mind takes the anger, not as a finished response, but as a compound of energy to *refract*. Without the mental refraction process, our energy is the expression of our raw animal heritage before the uniquely human brain evolved. If we snatch a slice of meat from a dog's dish while he is eating, we run the risk of being bitten. If we feel insulted, do we "instinctively" bite back? Or do we refract and reflect? Because we are a species more or less in "perpetual heat," do we yield to sexual impulse "instinctively"? What do we do *with* it? What do we do *about* it?

We are an army of impulses, but even an army becomes dysfunctional without order, planning, and restraint. If activated, our human brain helps us refract by perceiving a spectrum of different interpretations. The activated brain also helps us generate new options so that we can act wisely rather than react blindly. Refraction, then, is not mere reaction but a response. That is, we are personally *respons*-able for our actions.

Like the heart, the brain can function well or poorly. Ideally, the brain is an unsurpassed interplay of activities. Two of the most crucial activities are analysis and imagination working together so closely that imagination becomes a necessary aspect of analysis. New explanations and hypotheses become essential when we detect flaws in earlier explanations. We need a powerful imagination to *invent* new conjectures and improvements of our plans. In my experience as a therapist, I had to learn that many of my clients had developed lazy imaginations. Thinking that resolutions would appear magically, they became stuck, spinning their wheels in the same rut, having failed to *imagine* new plans, new approaches, new possibilities, and new opportunities. Thinking is an activity, not an aimless river that flows only where the boundaries permit. It is an ongoing process generating promising explanations or plans, and then revising them to make them better.

Learning from Ourselves and Others. We don't give toddlers complete freedom to do what they want. Nor do we say, "Let them learn for themselves the danger of playing in the heavy street traffic." If direct personal experience were their only way of learning, their mortality rate would soar. Children have to learn a great deal from the experiences of those who lived many years before them. Much of what we have learned and found useful for guiding our lives came from people who died long before we were born. Language, for example, came handed down through many generations. While we help modify it slightly, most of it arrived as an inheritance from people we have never met.

Toddlers depend on mature people who have discovered by trial and error that some choices are dangerous if not lethal. Most human thinking is by trial and error. Being smart is primarily learning from the trials, errors, and successes of others. A boy who had recently learned to drive ran over his little sister and killed her. That was his personal tragedy and his sister's. Unless we are hard-core sociopaths, we can certainly sympathize with him. We can put ourselves somewhat into his situation and feel some of his terrible anguish and remorse. By doing that, we can learn from his painful experience. He will not likely repeat the tragedy because he now knows that some of his decisions can carry consequences that last for many years, sometimes for life.

In a relatively free society, we can learn and profit from not only the mistakes of others, but also their successes. Instead of begrudging their skills and achievements, we take pleasure in them and use them as models and sources of encouragement. Rather than building our lives around the resentment for others, we imaginatively borrow some of their insights and expertise while emotionally identifying with their accomplishments. They, in turn, might find a way to share in our accomplishments and learn from us.

RESURGE

Our Biologchemical Roots and More. "Resurge" means to rise again to life, to activity, or to prominence. Our minds must resurge to prominence if we tend to survive and thrive well in diverse circumstances that sometimes change with surprising suddenness. Amid all the impulses, varied interests, passions, and drives that help form who we are, the human mind is the captain of the ship. Granted the conscious and deliberate thinking that we call "the mind" is not the whole person, without it human personhood would never come into being. If the mind is held captive by the impulses in their excess and disregard of one another, they will destroy the cooperation that holds the human body together to produce a person.

Human personhood with the human brain has its own "natural" dispositions and traits that have deep and special biochemical roots. While the new-born body is receiving reinforcement from outside itself, each of the bodily parts is contributing to the health and operation of all the other parts. But these biological roots and parts are not yet enough to create a person. When the human infant is delivered from one womb, it must enter another, the essential "social womb." The values and tender care from parents, relatives, friends, teachers, and others help constitute this social womb. The nourishments provided by it are as important as the milk and other foods that feed the infant's body and brain. The family and other institutions of the social womb mutually support one

10

another to provide a safe and caring social environment for the child. Just as physical bodies sometimes break down, so the social context can become dysfunctional. Ideally, all the "parts" of the body and the social context work together like a great orchestra.

In handling unruly and difficult issues, the mind must *resurge* to do its essential work because human beings are not preprogrammed at birth to live by mere instinct alone within the particular community they happen to have been born. More than any other species, human beings are dependent on the family for a very long period of time. This is partly because the human brain after birth still needs much more time to grow.

Cultures and subcultures differ significantly regarding the norms and expectations to which the children must adapt. A century ago in a farm community, many young American women in their *early* teens were having sex because they were married and expected to begin raising children. By the time a woman turned thirty, she might have given birth to five or even eight children. Today, a young man and woman in their teens are biologically ready for sexual intercourse. But their social and cultural world does not need teen-agers giving birth to children. Instead of performing a community service, pregnant teen-agers place an unnecessary hardship on both the children and on the caring community. The point is that sexual intercourse is more than a biological act. It carries profound emotional, economic, and moral consequences.

Thus, a crucial question emerges. Since our impulses carry far-reaching and diverse consequences, who is responsible for dealing with the consequences? What is the cost emotionally, vocationally, and financially? What are the moral consequences, for example, of bringing children into the world without the means to care for them? In short, the sexual impulse is profoundly different from the impulse to play tennis. Tennis anyone? Sex anyone?

The mind's prism discloses the diverse aspects of sexual intercourse to let us see that it *always carries a vast range of expectations*. This does not imply, however, that the to participants will agree on the same list of expectations. Ordinarily, when one tennis player does not live up to the other's expectations or she fails to communicate her abilities and intentions, the consequences are socially insignificant. Culturally and socially, the tennis stakes are comparatively low. Since there is no universal biological drive to play tennis, societies are under no great pressure to deal with it and its consequences. By contrast, the powerful biological drive to have sexual intercourse is universal and transcultural. Furthermore, since it does have long-term social and cultural consequences affecting the lives of many people, societies have been forced to adopt rules for dealing with it. In some societies, individuals may adopt additional personal rules and guidelines for their sexuality. Conflicts and disappointments surface when individuals have different personal sexual codes and expectations. The conflicts intensify when one partner fails to communicate his or her code and expectations. In some cases, one partner may slip into vagueness in order to hide in ambivalence. Or he or she might knowingly engage in miscommunication in order to mislead the other.

Communicating with Yourself. Sometimes, the big job is to communicate to yourself what you truly want for yourself, how you *feel* about various matters, and what you accept as your primary *responsibilities* to those with whom you have either an intimate or necessary relationship. Can you spell out the major elements of intimacy? Mentally, we surge to ask such a question because of self-interest. For example, what realistic expectations are involved in an intimate relationship? Do I want to cultivate those expectations with their corresponding responsibilities? Can I afford them emotionally and in other ways? Is such an intimacy a realistic possibility at this stage in my life? What will its impact be on my other relationships? Are there degrees of intimacy that can be articulated? In short, what am I getting myself into? How much delusional thinking am I experiencing?

We readily recognize that work on a job or committee takes *time*. To be of practical value, the work of thinking about our impulses and more critical personal issues must take time. Just as board members block off time to listen to one another if they intend to fulfill their missions, so each of us needs to plan to listen regularly to himself or herself. Our mind resurges to set the time for the inner board meetings and, in most cases, to announce the most critical agenda.

Second, the meeting must close the door, turn off the phones, and focus on the agenda's specifics. If one impulse seems to have taken over the personality, the other impulses and interests at the mental table must surge as a unit to create order. Some impulses bully the others. You in your role as the board director can say, "We are here to come to an agreement. If one impulse among us flies out of control, then we are all in deep trouble. We have to pull ourselves together as one. Some of our impulses here are so destructive to the rest of us that we might have to suppress them."

Over the years, most of us have worked out a measure of balance and harmony among our impulses. Some outlaw impulses are dangerous, however, and must be constrained mildly or severely--depending on how much they enrich the rest of the personality or how much they undermine the whole person. Some impulses can liquidate all the others and in the process exterminate itself. Better to suppress or sublimate them before they capture the whole personality. In some ways, an addiction is an impulse or a craving that threatens to take over the whole person. It builds its own army against rest of our drives, goals, and interests. Unless restrained, it will capture the whole person and use it like a tool to satisfy itself alone. So, know your enemy--the enemy within, the internal egotist that uses the other impulses and contributes to overall misery. Assemble yourself at your own interior board meeting and let every aspect of yourself *acknowledge* that at least one of your cunning, restless members intends to take over the whole person and put it to work for itself without pay. More on addiction later.

Mistakes and the Power of Honest Thinking. Most people are so good at recognizing their mistakes and correcting them that they do not need to dwell on the process. Jane realized she just ran a red light. "Guilty. No excuses. Next time, heed the red light! I don't want to cause a serious accident."

Helena now believes she married the wrong man. Some mistakes have to be looked in the eye. In this case, think about why it is a mistake. If it really is a mistake, how did she make such a bad choice? Would she repeat it? Can it be corrected by marriage counseling? Possibly.

Divorce? Possible. This major decision requires a major conference with the whole self. Several conferences will be necessary. Would divorcing her husband be a bigger mistake? Helena wonders if she is engaging in wishful thinking about her life after the divorce. What does the marriage cost her emotionally, financially, and otherwise? What is the cost of living with him? Hard questions take time to sort out. There is no simple calculator for weighing the pros and cons.

We inevitably make mistakes because our knowledge is limited and our judgment imperfect. If you could have avoided certain mistakes but made them nevertheless, don't try to justify them. Don't switch to the passive voice by saying, "Mistakes were made" as if there was no subject. Be accurate. "*I* am the subject. *I* made the mistake." If someone you admire made a mistake, admit it. Don't rationalize. Learn from his or her mistakes, as well as your own. Rationalizing and making excuses are themselves mistakes.

Say to yourself, "How do I get out of this mess in a responsible way?" At your inner conference, talk calmly to yourself about ways to avoid repeating the more serious mistakes. If you have a level-headed, fully trustworthy friend, you might bring him or her in on your personal board meeting. But do not turn the decision over to your friend. Her or she is your consultant. *Your* mind is the director of the board.

In Control and Out of Control. Consider the following scene in which you are the major protagonist. Someone walks up to you and says, "Hello. Remember me? I once worked for you. Served you well when you needed me, but it was only part-time work. So, now I'm taking over."

"What do you mean, you're taking over?"

"You've been running your life, using my service when it suited you. But things are gonna be different. Leave it all to me. Now, here's the way things are going—"

"Hey, just a minute! You show up and just assume you can take control when *you* decide?"

"Right. I'm now in the driver's seat. You're merely along for the ride."

"Who do you think you are, anyhow?"

"Me? You gotta be kidding. You've known me since you were a child. So, don't pretend I'm a stranger. When I began reading the signs, so to speak, I decided you were placidly inviting me to take command. When a major crisis became too big for you to deal with, or when things didn't go your way, you began calling on me more and more."

"You're off your rocker. I don't even know you."

"Don't insult my intelligence. I've lost track of the times you gave me the cue to rush in on the scene to take control. Well, from now on, I'll decide when to make my entrance and take charge. From now on, the roles around here will be reversed. I'm no longer your servant; you are my servant."

"Bull! Nobody's going to—"

"Ha! Look at you—losing it, aren't you. You really don't recognize me, do you? I'm already at the helm while you're so pathetic in self-management that you can't even keep track of yourself. I'm your former servant. Anger! Yep, I'm your beloved Anger. You can call me Mr. Rage. This life you've been calling yours is no longer yours. You've turned it over to me!"

Some people have waked to discover they had been turning their lives over to Anger or some undermining impulse. They began to suspect they are no longer in control of their lives when Anger seemed to step out of its proper but limited role. Upon reflection, they had to admit that their Anger or some other impulse appeared at the wrong time to carry its service to excess, creating embarrassing or even dangerous situations. Some people have waked to discover a hostile takeover. They no longer enjoy the self-control they thought they had.

Vivian Holmes began to suspect she was losing some of her self-management skills when friends, family members, and business associates no longer sat down with her to discuss matters calmly and rationally. She felt strange about herself. At times, she seemed no longer Vivian but someone who looked like her. In some respects, she had *invented her own replacement*. In critical moments of frustration, she had summoned Anger to the forefront, relinquishing more and more of her self-identity. She was in effect saying, "Let Anger deal with the frustrating conflicts. Let Anger resort to intimidation rather than respectful conversation and intelligent negotiation."

Anger is the kind of emotion that has no self-regulator. You control it; or it controls you. If not controlled by you the owner, it will turn on your friends and even turn on you. Anger often veers toward self-ruin unless checked. In the worst scenarios, Anger can take control of your reasoning skills and use them to transform you into a methodical engine of revenge either against others or against yourself. Long ago, psychiatrist Karl Manning provided case studies of individuals whose anger or unexamined guilt turned on them in very subtle but harmful ways.

Anger can be compared to a watchdog that you take with you on a walk. You have the end of the leash firmly in your grip. Your dog sometimes barks when he thinks you are threatened or encroached upon. He is a useful dog, provided, of course, you still have your dog-anger in your control. If you come under physical attack, your dog-anger will help defend you. On the other hand, *you*—not your Anger—are responsible for keeping yourself out of threatening situations. By having more common sense than your Anger, you possess the possibility of preventing impulsiveness from leading you into situations that will place you in danger or in a compromising situation. If you do not exercise caution, your anger can quickly crate a serious crisis. This is like letting your dog lead you into an environment where there are other dogs who feel threatened. If you are not in control of your anger, it could lead you into something comparable to a dogfight, or worse. Out of control, it can get you injured or killed—a loved one severely injured. Uncontrolled anger can ruin a friendship, destroy a marriage, sink a career, turn a law-abiding citizen into a criminal, a surgeon into a butcher, or a teacher into a sarcastic bully.

An Alarm System. Is anger an aspect of our human nature that can and should be deleted? Would we be better off if all anger could be removed by an emotional lobotomy? Or does it have a proper and useful role?

Like guilt, overwhelming impulses may be compared to an alarm system. If the house fills with smoke, the alarm enacts as a warning signal suggesting that something has gone wrong. Unfortunately, impulses can sometimes be imprecise or misleading. Some people became alarmed over matters that require no action. In most cases, it is useful to turn off the alarm so that we may take control and make rational decisions. Impulses have no ready switches that can be flipped. They must be directed by thought, skill, and technique. Those most successful in dealing anger and other undermining impulses have discovered that in most situations, the impulse is their own *invention*. Far from lying out there like a serpent in tall grass or a bear in the bushes, the impulse comes into being by the individual's act of creation.

John is a truck mechanic who has been working at his trade for years. He knows he is a good mechanic, but a customer says to him, "Mister, you aren't a real mechanic. You're an incompetent who just tinkers with motors." Upon hearing this, John need not respond by becoming angry. He has several options, each of which is an invention or an activity on his part. Instead of creating an angry response, he can calmly walk away and engage in another activity. Or he can create another response, namely, thinking. He reminds himself that he is the one in charge of his own self-inventions. Shakespeare and the philosopher Georg Hegel help us understand that to be a person is to become a work of art, a creation in process.

The Artist. If you are a work of art, who is the artist? According to Hegel and Shakespeare, *you* are. Your genes and social environment, including your parents, have provided the material; but you do the creating.

Freud did not claim that parents make their children who they are. The goal of psychoanalysis as he practiced it was that of helping his clients gain insight into the ways they had used the conditions and circumstances of their childhood and youth to create their personalities up to the time that they walked into his office. Just as painters and musicians have different styles and techniques, so each of us has a personal technique and style of self-creation. Just as artists and musicians can improve their techniques, so we cam improve our techniques and skills for self-creation.

The offspring of wealthy parents have sometimes turned themselves into spoiled brats who never became mature adults. To justify their failures, they concocted the convenient lie that parents predetermine what their children will become. Hence, they as their offspring have no responsibility for becoming who they are. Shakespeare lets us see that characters do not unfold as if they were rolled up with rugs with all the designs and shapes already imprinted on them. Rather, human characters develop by reinventing themselves, taking whatever they receive and using it to shape themselves. Hamlet not only eavesdrops on others, he also eavesdrops on himself. He overhears himself and then has the opportunity to learn from his past decisions just as an artist can step back and look at what she has painted to determine whether the work on canvas is what she had envisioned. Beethoven's notebooks for the Ninth Symphony's last movement show that the introduction to the movement tells the story of his struggles to solve a problem. Musicians and artists often struggle to solve issues that develop out of their drive to create something worthy of the ideal they have envisioned. To create better approximations to our goals, we often encounter frustrating obstacles and challenges that present the option of becoming angry, which may divert us from our initial goal. Our energy goes into creating anger and then feeding it.

Most creative living involves trial and error. Dealing creatively with destructive, self-defeating impulsiveness is often a process of trial and error. The trick, however, is to learn as quickly as possible from the trials and errors of others, both those who have failed and those who have succeeded. One of the most successful techniques for dealing with impulsiveness is to stop feeding it. But is that not like asking someone to stop thinking about an albino pig? Imagine someone saying, "I'll give you ten thousand dollars if you can avoid thinking about the ten thousand dollars for the next fifteen minutes." Assuming you are honest, could you meet the requirements?

We feed anger by dwelling on the insult or whatever we choose to label as "the cause." Those who successfully counter anger, however, have developed the technique of turning their thoughts and feelings to *something more interesting than the anger*. To stop thinking about the albino pig or the ten thousand dollars, our minds would need to focus on something else, something compelling and involving. Many impulses in addition to anger can be dealt with by developing the technique of becoming quickly engrossed in other thoughts or other activities.

Active Thinking. By thinking about something interesting, we give ourselves the advantage of deciding whether we will feed our impulse or nourish our anger. Thinking is movement that quickly goes in search of reliable alternatives to anger and impulsiveness. A reliable alternative is a *captivating activity* that at the very least is a harmless replacement of the impulse that would undermine our long-term freedom.

In many cases, any harmless action will serve to replace the impulsive option as long as it is sufficiently engrossing. When John the mechanic hears what could be interpreted as an insult directed at him, he might find it difficult to just stop having angry thoughts and feelings. That is because merely *stopping* the mind from thinking is not itself an act. Angry thinking or impulsive reactions can better be countered by *doing* something harmless or *thinking* about something exciting. To say we have trouble controlling anger may be a way of saying we need to invent alternative thoughts, images, or positive actions. We often stop anger by shifting our thoughts to beautiful scenes, interesting people, or compelling ideas that can compete with anger. Something must *fascinate* us long enough to overshadow our impulse.

Alternatives. Let's say you are angry because someone at your workplace is unscrupulously promoting himself or herself at your expense. You feel manipulated. You generate anger that might be justified or partially justified. Your alarm has gone off. You feel cheated, and you think this unscrupulous person in a genuine threat to your career. What can you do?

First, like a painter, you can step back and critically examine your assessment of the situation. You want to be accurate in identifying the precise actions that are creating trouble for you. What is the trouble-making person doing to you—precisely. A painter pauses to examine what he has on the canvas before he proceeds to correct or improve it. Like painting or composing music, thinking often takes time. That is because in thinking, you often examine the situation from different angles. Try looking at it from the angle of someone whose judgment you respect. It is also useful to talk with a friend or a trustworthy person who might help you either uncover facts you have overlooked or interpret the facts with a different slant. This trustworthy person might be of considerable help if he or she is calm, rational, and sympathetic. Make a list of individuals you could phone and talk with. Hone the list. In short, do not sit and stew in anger juices. Plan ahead to cut anger off at the pass.

Second, in talking with that friend or sympathetic relative, don't generalize. Calmly sort out the relevant facts from the irrelevant facts. Is your career really in danger? If it is, what are the *specific* actions that create the danger? Urge your friend to help you to avoid grandiose emotions or theatrics that leave you nursing your anger rather than pinpointing the critical areas that need to be faced. This is comparable to smelling smoke in the house or hearing the smoke alarm and then moving quickly to locate the fire in case it is small enough to extinguish quickly and effectively. Like fire, anger can sometimes spread rapidly and indiscriminately unless quickly checked. One of the most successful checks on anger is a dose of alternatives plans and images, which must not be confused with hurling arguments at the person with whom you are angry. Arguments projected in anger are notoriously ineffective in improving the other person's thoughts or actions. Becoming argumentative is only dousing the flame with kerosene.

REORGANIZE

I'm one of my best teachers. But I have to take time to listen to me. I need to pay attention and ask useful questions. Some of the questions are embarrassing or difficult to ask. But I need to ask them and then listen patiently. Sometimes, as my own teacher, I don't have a good answer. So, like a good teacher, I try to find the answer. A good teacher is good partly because he or she has had the patience to learn from other teachers. In any case, I need to listen more carefully when I'm teaching myself.

I have an acquaintance who can talk about twenty different subjects in five minutes but say nothing enlightening on any of them. He isn't so much a developed personality as a crisscross of momentary impulses. When I'm in conference with myself, I try to remain focused and to stay on the subject. I show respect by expecting the exchange to be useful and meaningful.

DIFFERENCES. Human cultures can be strikingly different from one another. Try imagining who you would be had you been born in Saudi Arabia and had lived there until now. To what extent would you be the same person you are today? Would the differences be so significant that you would literally be another person? One of my colleague's friends told him that her husband was not the same man she had married. When people in their sixties go to their high school

21

reunions, do they instantly recognize one another? In many cases, the beliefs and personality changes may be more profound than the conspicuous physical changes. Furthermore, just as people are different from each other, so in time each of us might become different from himself. It is important to accept—or at least recognize—that we are different in various ways.

A MEANINGFUL LIFE. To relate sensitively and intelligently to people, we need at times to reorganize certain pockets of our thinking. For example, in our pluralistic society, we cannot afford to ignore the fact that individuals may differ markedly as to what they regard as a meaningful life. What for one person is a fulfilling way of living might be for another a miserable existence. What you regarded as a meaningful life when you were twenty might appear wearisome when you are thirty. Donald cannot understand how people outside his religion can bear to face life's problems day after day. By contrast, Jason regards Donald's religion as absurd and cannot understand why he would remain involved in it. We are often tempted to make strong judgments about people who hold to certain beliefs greatly different from our own. Instead of pondering the pros and cons of the beliefs themselves, we hastily judge that something must be severely wrong with those who believe them. We dismiss the individuals as psychologically underdeveloped, morally deficient, or intellectually barren. We hastily say Marlene is a Methodist because she never developed to full adulthood. Or Carl is an atheist because he suffers from an arrogance that is a compensation for suffering from humiliation in childhood. Or Stan is an anti-evolution creationist because he is intellectually challenged.

We face also the temptation to conclude that when someone holds to certain views that we regard as severely flawed, all his other views are unworthy of consideration. To make this hast generalization, we deny ourselves the possibility of learning anything from this person. Very likely, most of us embrace at least a few beliefs that are at best highly questionable. If your electrician holds to certain political views that appear far-fetched, do you assume that he cannot wire your house properly?

MEANINGS OF MEANINGFUL. I will briefly explore ways in which people have described their lives as meaningful. I do not intend to evaluate or judge the ways, but to bring them out in clear view so we can better understand them. Since many, if not most, members of our species desire a meaningful life, it will be useful to understand why some regard a particular way or style as deeply meaningful *to them.*

1. ***Membership.*** Most of us want to belong to a group. Juanita suffered depression when everything seemed to be going well for her. When her friend Lyn learned that Juanita had rotated off a committee, Lyn congratulated her for being "free" of the responsibility. Later, she learned that Juanita believed she had contributed significantly to the community through the committee. What would have been an increase in Lyn's freedom proved to be a serious loss for Juanita. Just as a word gains added meaning in its broader context, so individuals feel more meaningful when they belong to the appropriate social context. When individuals for various reasons leave their families and its network of supports, they often seek out a group that offers important reinforcement. Finding a genuinely constructive community becomes a practical problem. What would be a useless social bond for one individual might be profoundly meaningful to another. In working with other people, we need to be sensitive to the importance of membership and its contribution to what they regard as a meaningful life. In working closely with others, we might avoid fruitless conflict or hostility if we recognize our thinking by stepping imaginatively into their skin to become them for a while. Admittedly, this is risky; for when we return to our own skin, we might not see things exactly as we previously had. Not to venture outside our own perspective, on the other hand, is to risk becoming mentally stunted or emotionally encapsulated.

Some people we work with do not want to be understood beyond narrow confines. They want their privacy respected and have no wish to be known except in their roles on the job, committee, or board. They prefer recognition from us to be confined to the task at hand. It is an art to separate (1) your working closely with someone on a problem from (2) your becoming involved in their lives. The distinction is crucial.

2. ***A Sense of Control.*** To have a meaningful life, everyone wants control of certain aspects of his or her life. To be in direct control of every aspect of your life is impossible. Not even the greatest surgeon in town would consider doing major surgery on his own knee. She would want to select the surgeon and perhaps those assisting in the surgery room. Unless she is a "control freak," she might trust her husband to select the trees to plant on their property or the best voice teacher for their daughter.

Members of the work team usually prefer to be in charge of different aspects of the project. Conflict arises when two or more insist on making the major and final decisions of the department or committee. The role of a mediator can sometimes increase efficiency and reduce disruptive conflict.

Cornelius came into his history department at the university as a significant addition to the department. Gradually, several of his colleagues realized that he behaved as if he had been invited to become the guiding for or the key member of the department. Coming with his own agenda, he treated the department meetings as a forum for implementing his own agenda. The idea of a mutual exchange among colleagues of equal competence seemed alien to him.

The function of the chairperson of a department, board, or committee may sometimes be that of dealing with prima donnas or self-appointed stars who have not grasped the elementary fact that no one is the entire show or team. An actor with a minor part finds meaning and personal fulfillment in perfecting his or her role and thus adding to the entire performance. Many people see their lives as parts in "the great drama of life." For them, "the meaning of life" is to execute their role in life to the best of their abilities even when under adverse circumstance. They can accept their endurance of inevitable hardships as meaningful just because they perceive the hardships as a scene in the greater drama and as essential to their part in the production. While they cannot control the entire drama, they can control their own daily performance and take great pride and satisfaction in it.

3. ***Orientation.*** Change is common in some cultures. When change comes too quickly or drastically, we can become slightly disoriented or

perhaps traumatized. Reorganization of thinking and activity becomes imperative if we are to make creative use of the changes. Industrial, technological, institutional, or cognitive changes may evoke fear or a sense of meaninglessness. An individual might say, "I don't know what it all means now," "I don't know what I'm supposed to do now," "I no longer know what to believe," "Nothing makes sense." Counselors and therapists sometimes serve as coaches to help clients learn new "plays" for the new game in town. When a major change occurs on the job, fellow workers can sometimes communicate their apprehension calmly while working out new guidelines and responsibilities. They can make clear the new expectations, new assignments, and new difficulties. This is the time for understanding and encouragement. Unexpected reorganization imposed upon coworkers will require them to reexamine their plans, attitudes, and directions. In some cases, coworkers discover a new appreciation of their collective ability to deal with the crisis.

Much of human life runs by habits that have served us well. We rely on a great mental library of countless scripts for making many of our most important decisions. Each of us is both a conservative and a liberal. The conservative aspect says, "Let's not presume that everyone before us was a fool. Use the scripts that we inherited from our wisest ancestors. Don't try to reinvent the wheel. Accept the guidance of those who struggled before us. Learn from them." Our liberal aspect says, "Don't assume our ancestors were infallible. Their wisdom must be adapted to the changes, good and bad, that come our way. Let's respect our ancestors by using our hard-won intelligence just as they used their hard-won intelligence." Rearrangement or reorientation is often hard work. It does not drop down from the blue. We need to learn from both the wondrous accomplishments and terrible mistakes of our predecessors.

4. ***Sources of Enjoyment.*** Few people can find a meaningful life void of enjoyment. When people say they no longer find meaning in life, they often reveal that their reliable sources of fulfillment, satisfaction, or pleasure have been severely curtailed. Later, I will deal with the theme of *enjoyment* and *pleasure* in some detail. Since a major portion of our waking hours are devoted to work, we count ourselves fortunate

if some of those hours provide satisfaction and pleasure. Jean realized that working with one of her colleagues had been a major source of her enjoyment on the job. When her friend Helen died, Jean missed her more than she had realized. She resolved to become a friend to Helen's replacement. That did not work out. By chance, however, she discovered that another work colleague, Natalie, missed Helen terribly. They gained comfort in talking about Helen and gradually found they had more in common than they had realized. Jean and Natalie made a point also of introducing their husbands to each other. That proved to be a major increase in their overall pleasure. Although their job sometimes threw them in competition with one another, Natalie and Jean understood the need of maintaining an atmosphere of friendliness and humor, if not cheerfulness, especially during the times of unexpected job pressures.

Equally important is being on the "right" committee or with the "right" group. While one person will find serving on a particular committee or board to be fulfilling, her friend might find it stressful if not exceedingly boring. When Bill and Zack realized they were on the "wrong" committees, their perceptive supervisor let them exchange.

It is often possible to invent harmless ways of bringing more satisfaction and enjoyment to the job, the committee, or the board meeting. Some business firms have discovered that workers who find satisfaction in major aspects of their work tend to be more efficient. Such satisfaction makes the work *intrinsically* meaningful to them. When workers or committee members feel they have more input into the decision-making process, their satisfaction level rises. We want our work to "count for something." The more it does, the more integrated the work becomes to our lives and personalities.

Every job has "a dishwashing aspect," but even that can sometimes be couched in good humor or other ways that reduce the pressure or boredom.

In a Detroit company where certain automobile parts were made, a college student, Matthew, became a summer employee at a physically difficult job. Matthew discovered that two of the regular workers became angry frequently when one or more of the bumper guards fell of the racks during the process of cleaning and plating them. The workers, including Matthew, had to use a metal rod to dip into the barrels and tanks to fish out the fallen guards. The workers asked Matthew why he never became angry when his guards fell off. Only later did he understand that he had quickly determined that a certain number of the guards would inevitably fall off each day and would need to be retrieved. He did not become angry because the process of fishing out the fallen guards was a part of his job, as he perceived it. He had quickly reorganized his expectations to fit the reality of the job. His lack of anger made him more efficient.

Many years later, he wondered if his two coworkers became angry on the job because they believed they would be stuck in the difficult job for many years, if not for the rest of their lives. Matthew knew he would return to college at the end of the summer. After working at the Detroit company for a summer and learning more about the reality of hard work, he reorganized his thoughts and habits regarding his college studies in the fall. He perceived his college work in a different light, found it more rewarding than the summer job, and became a more serious student. At the same time, his studies became more interesting and enjoyable to him. Many unexpected sources of pleasure often await those who do not tie themselves up in unrealistic expectations.

5. *Recognition.* Individuals have gone to therapists because some aspect of their personality or life needed to be recognized. Although a thief will ordinarily not want to be recognized as a thief, he or she wants recognition for something. Imagine living an entire month in which your friends and family see you and know who you are, but they don't really see you. You aren't recognized as a person with your personal needs and goals. A mother complained that her family would miss her because of what she did for them. "But they don't recognize me as anyone other than a bundle of functions that make their lives easier." A football star that received recognition as a great player needed also recognition as a father and husband. "I'm more than a football celebrity." Being sensitive to others requires not only emotional empathy, but also the kind of intellectual empathy that allows us to think somewhat from the perspective of the other person.

Dr. Lawton became quite dissatisfied with his job as a university faculty member. He suffered because he felt he no longer had his department's respect and recognition. The university had the policy of "publish or teach more courses." Lawton chose to write fewer articles and papers, which meant he no longer competed with most of his colleagues. According to the rule, those who published received a lighter teaching load. Because Lawton ceased to publish, the department increased his teaching load.

Lawton began to feel his work was meaningless, and he complained to a colleague in another department, who suggested that he reorganize his thinking and expectations. "Look," said the friend, "you still have a splendid job. Sure, it's a heavier teaching load, but you're an excellent teacher. Furthermore, you travel abroad every summer and spend other weeks abroad during the year. So, why are you complaining? Imagine yourself trying to teach high school students instead of college students. That would be a much more difficult job, and it would pay you a smaller salary. So, enjoy your career here at the university. Enjoy your life. You're doing quite well!"

Lawton's problem lay primarily in his failure to reorganize his expectations. Although a bright, effective teacher, he neglected to think through his situation. Unable to see himself as his colleagues saw him, he mistakenly thought they had denigrated him. In reality, they simply followed the rules. They recognized him as a remarkable teacher. Since he no longer published, he could not expect to be recognized as a persistent writer. He did not revise his thinking sufficiently to appreciate his good fortune in having an enviable position at the university. His friend urged him to become more realistic so that he could continue to experience the *joy* of teaching.

To be sure, grading student papers is scarcely a peak experience. It can be the dishwashing aspect of the job. But performing before a classroom of college students can be an abiding pleasure that carries also wonderful memories of impacting the lives of some students for years to come. In June 2008, for example, a professor in Texas received an email from his former student in Chili to tell him that his novel had won in a literary contest and to thank the professor for having an important influence on him in 1991.

Much misery comes from making no realistic connection between our expectations and our actions. Lawton failed to ask, "What can I expect from not publishing in journals or presenting papers as professional meetings? By not following the explicit guidelines, why would I expect to receive a lighter teaching load? Are my expectations realistic?"

5. ***Service to Others.*** Whether on the job, committee, board, or in the family, an egotistical person loses one of the major elements of a meaningful life by being unstable to *share in the accomplishments and joys of others*. When Carla realized others had helped her in countless ways, she discovered also that she was in effect expressing her gratitude by living a meaningful life and helping others to enrich their lives too. It was as if the beautiful song her mother had sung to her was now a song in the heart and on the lips of the granddaughter. The American philosopher expressed this sentiment simply and profoundly.

We who now live are parts of a humanity extends into the remote past.... The things in civilization we most prize are not of ourselves. They exist by grace of the doings and sufferings of the continuous human community in which you are a link. Ours is the responsibility of conserving, transmitting, rectifying and expanding the heritage of values we have received that those who come after us may receive it more solid and secure, more widely accessible and more generously shared than we have received it. Here are all the elements for a religious faith that shall not be confined to sect, class, or race. Such a faith has always been implicitly the common faith of mankind.

How to Recognize and Relate to a Sociopath

1. A word of caution is necessary. We do not want to become paranoid, thinking everyone who strongly disagrees with us or has done us harm is a sociopath. At the same time, not everyone who appears congenial and helpful is what he or she appears to be. We want to be neither unduly distrustful nor tragically naïve.

2. Sociopaths are ***greatly different*** from most people, although they seem to be like us in almost every way until we get to know them. They

often marry and have a family. They can talk smoothly, say the right things, and be interesting. They look like us and can appear friendly and caring. In reality, they care little for others because they have no positive attachment to others. They can fake love and compassion but not experience it. Void of conscience, they regard others as objects to be used and cleverly manipulated. Life appears to them to be a game. In reality, they are quite prepared to lie, cheat, or steal in order to win. Some commit murder. Real games have rules that the contestants on both sides respect. Sociopaths have no regard for impartial rules. They will invoke rules when doing so serves their purpose.

3. Void of conscience, sociopaths can experience shame at being caught, but they do not experience guilt. They can use the guilt of others to *manipulate* them, but they suffer no pangs of guilt. While we might offer some *explanations* as to how individuals became sociopaths, we would be foolish to assume their behavior should be *excused*.

4. The sociopath's major weapon for controlling others is *deceit*. With lies and duplicity, they worm their way into your life in order to use you. Do not try to relate to a sociopath as if he were potentially a decent person who can be helped. In short, pay close attention to discrepancies, inconsistencies, and promises that seem too good to be true or that casually glide over common sense and common decency. Do not share secrets or your private life with anyone who is too casual regarding the truth. Cunning and the smooth twisting of the truth are the sociopath's meant and drink. They build your defeat with the bricks of their fabrications. Do not give them a penny of your earnings. Do not share your work with them unless you want to be cheated. Give them no affection unless you intend to be made a fool of or worse. Do not allow your politeness to be used against you.

5. Sociopaths would like to make it easy for you to *violate your conscience* for some presumably superior purpose, to use your conscience as a tool to his advantage, not yours. Do not let him toy with it. If you have trusted her by giving her the benefit of the doubt, accept calmly that you made a mistake. Do not try to justify it. Above all, do not repeat it. Learn quickly from the mistake.

6. *Flattery* is not a compliment, but a falsehood. It is a part of

the sociopath's style. If you need flattery, try to overcome the need. Grandiosity, exaggerations, and promises that tap into our vulnerability and fantasies make us a target for the sociopath, who is basically anti-social despite his sincere-sounding talk. He or she feeds on the gullible and those desperate for even the appearance of a glowing compliment. The sociopath will use charm or fear—whichever works—to manipulate others. The best way to relate to sociopaths is to have no relations at all with them. Unfortunately, our jobs sometimes place us with them. If our job requires working with a sociopath, we must never yield to magical thinking or believing that we have some remarkable gift of transforming the sociopath into a caring, respectful human being. In short, we must not con ourselves or allow sociopaths to con us. On the job, we do well to keep all relationships with him or her to the absolute minimum. We must avoid raising false hopes by expecting some magical transformation to take place.

7. Genuine, long-term cooperation is foreign to the anti-social individual. The only relationship of importance to him or her is ***his dominance and your submission***. No matter how subtle, smooth, and clever their approach to us, sociopaths do not think in terms of mutuality an elementary respect, although some of them are consummate actors. They excel in hypocrisy.

Among their deepest fears is that of losing control of the situation. They are prone to regard your good will as an opening for doing you harm and giving themselves an edge.

8. Compassion, sympathy, and mercy are qualities that help ordinarily make a relationship and a society sane and enjoyable. Sociopaths sometimes find it expedient to ***play on our compassion and pity*** by pressing the right buttons, using tears if necessary, embroidered tales of woe or other half-truths to abuse our kindness. It is wrong to waste compassion on sociopaths. A part of social responsibility is to direct compassion toward the helpless, those who deserve it now, or those who will eventually be able to pass the compassion on to others. Sociopaths need love, but they abuse and pollute it. Unable to offer love, they become amoral ink blotters or sponges absorbing the goodness of others. At best, they can extend only flashes of a love that is not basic

to their character. They cannot love because the relentless desire to use and dominate others lies at the core of who they are.

9. As a rule, we extend respect to those with whom we work and come into contact. This is essential to a civil and cordial society. Sociopaths *do not deserve our respect*. If a sociopath is an accomplished musician, we can admire and respect her work. But we do not admire her anti-social character and outlook. We would be wise to fear her. This is not to say that we disclose any of our fears to her. The point is to disclose to her as little as possible, to relate as little as possible. Rather than inform her that we regard her as a sociopath, we keep the flow of information to the bare essentials required by the goals of the committee, job, or board. Politeness is appropriate but not friendliness. Intrigue loves company. Sociopaths thrive on intrigue and cannot resist pulling others in with them. "Come in; the intrigue is fine," they say with their smiles, seductions, and enticements. Eventually, the intrigue approaches a sadomasochistic relationship—domination and submission.

10. Many sociopaths are also narcissistic with exaggerated claims of their powers and importance. Some demand glory and may give the air of possessing glory, power, or some other attributes lifting them to greatness and uniqueness. While craving unconditional love from others, they appear to believe their glory or greatness is their special contribution to those willing to bathe in it.

REHEARSE

In June 2008, Richard Thomas Wright ran out of gas a mile from the bank he had just robbed. His impulse to become temporarily rich in only minutes lacked the elementary forethought to purchase sufficient fuel for the getaway. "He must have forgotten to rehearse."

Practice. Even the greatest football players must practice and improve their skills. A quarterback usually has his personal coach to help him refine his skill. Great violinists know that after skipping days of practice, they have lost the finer edge of their art. One way to practice our skills for handling harmful impulsiveness is and destructive behavior is to rehearse things to do or say that take the focus away from the process by which the behavior takes control and spreads.

In some cases, quietly and politely walking away from conflict will reduce anger, *provided* the other person knows you will later return to address the issue calmly. If the other person does not, however, believe you will return, then your walking away may be viewed as a disrespectful or hostile act to cut the person off. When calm, we can practice dealing with frustrating or confronting situations by deliberately *setting aside time to rehearse alternative words and actions* that create a calm or more workable climate. Having imagined these alternatives, we privately rehearse some of them until they *become second nature*, a part of who we are. Some people dream up words that will match insult with insult. They dream up ways to put down the other person. By contrast, we can invent rational and appropriate responses that become so much a part of us that we do not need to pause to think, since *we have already spent considerable time in both imagining intelligent responses and practicing them* in our heads or before a mirror. No matter how good a professional quarterback is, he practices because he knows he will encounter situations that take him by surprise. His hours at practice help him reduce the number of times he will be taken totally by surprise.

Technique. Techniques and skills usually do not develop without rehearsal and practice. A carpenter improves by becoming aware of his own errors and by learning from those who have already mastered the carpentry trade. In the moments when you are calm and not impulsive, you can practice the soliloquy, that is, talk to yourself and privately recall the times when you invented and fed your harmful impulse rather than created a more practical response. This step, in return, creates greater time for gentle honesty. Rather than insult or berate yourself, you can gently point out that you do not want to describe yourself as an impetuous person. A basic part of your personal self-identity is your behavior. If you manifest a considerable amount of reckless or headless behavior, you are a reckless person. You are doubtless more than that, but your behavior cannot be treated as an alien being.

In times of gentle honesty, we will most likely acknowledge that we want to exude less impulsiveness and more self-possession. This gentle honesty becomes also a part of what we are becoming, keeping in mind that we are our own work of art. True, we do not create ourselves out of nothing. At the same time, the materials and ingredients that make up our conditions do not assemble themselves to create us. They have no creative power. We do. We create by selecting some of the materials available and using them creatively while also rejecting other materials and working to develop more useful materials. We go to school or become apprentices to develop better materials from which to create ourselves for tomorrow and all our other tomorrows.

Testing for Flaws. A great deal of thinking is rehearsal of our plans in the imagination to test them for serious flaws before we attempt to enact them. You are going for an important job interview next week. Aware that first impressions can carry considerable weight, you will dress appropriately, of course. Since you need this job, you have done some research and now know more of what will be required if you are offered the job and you take it.

The interview will be more than pro forma. You anticipate having to answer substantial questions, and you have deemed it wise to ask substantial questions of your own. To increase the probabilities that you will appear well organized and knowledgeable, you might either write down key questions and answers, or make notes and arrange them in useful order. You might even rehearse certain answers to anticipated questions. Another purpose of the rehearsal and preparation is to internalize the material to make your presentation fluent.

Rehearsal has advantages in other areas. Ricardo has changed jobs and is now going to work with cheerful people, whereas at his previous job cheerfulness was not an element of the ambiance. If cheerfulness is not natural to Ricardo, he might consider pleasantness. If he is ordinarily cheerful but does not wish to appear excessively or inappropriately cheerful at work or on the committee, he might rehearse being moderately pleasant. Smiling is more prevalent in some regions of North America than in other regions. Pleasantness would seem to be the safest way to begin. Teresa asked her new husband to postpone his singing immediately upon rising in the morning. He had to learn that his high-octane exuberance had to be moderated until his normally pleasant and thoughtful wife could adapt to it.

Just as we do not reveal certain thoughts and feelings to everyone at work or on the committees, so we do not disclose all our emotions indiscriminately. With some people we can joke; with others we remain pleasant but less outgoing. In *The Presentation of the Self in Everyday Life*, sociologist Erving Goffman speaks of "concealed practices that are incompatible with fostered impressions" (64). Far from recommending that each person lead a double life, he is suggesting that certain traits and activities be restrained.

It is one thing to say and do things that *mis*represent our abilities and our private feelings. It is another to keep various thoughts, feelings, and activities to ourselves. Just as we do not owe full disclosure of our bank account to anyone who asks for it, so we do not owe information about ourselves to just anyone. There are degrees of friendship, and the degree helps determine the information about ourselves we will or will not share with others.

Hypocrisy is openly professing to believe in and respect certain values that we do not believe in. we are morally weak perhaps when we fail to live by our values, but that does not make us hypocritical. In presenting ourselves, we invariably withhold many of our thoughts and feelings. We recognize that some behaviors are appropriate to one setting but inappropriate to others. In some cases, we have to do a mental rehearsal of our activities in the appropriate setting in order to become comfortable with the behavior, to make it more natural.

Since human beings do not live by rigid instincts alone, we have to develop a wide repertoire as though performing in many plays, each with its special cues, lines, and gestures. Furthermore, we perform on many stages and have to keep in mind which play we are in at the moment and who our audience is at the time. We have many roles to learn well. In most cases, each offers a range of responses so that we are not bound to a script cast in iron. At the same time, each role has its boundaries and controls that make it a genuine social role rather than mere random words and behavior.

At work, in marriage, and in other relationships, appropriate roles are essential.

Without them, human interchange would quickly become chaotic and perpetually frustrating. Roles make us more predictable without our becoming automations. Strange as it seems at first, the existence of roles in human society helps increase the level of freedom for the individual. More of this later when I discuss freedom.

In this context, to rehearse is to learn and feel at home in the roles that we assume. Make no mistake: we do assume roles. To be is to be enrolled. Whether we are a prisoner behind bars or a high school principal, each of our roles is a network of is a network of explicit and implicit expectations to be carried out under the appropriate circumstances—on the appointed stage. The wife of a department chairman at his college reminded him, "At home, Cal, you aren't the chairman."

Since we cannot live by our instincts alone, we must develop a workable gamut for each role. Rehearsal of the roles in a safe and accepting setting is, thus, both necessary and useful. The professor's wife acknowledged his important role as chairman at the university. At home, he had other roles, each with its special expectations. Until she expressed her observation, he had been delivering regal lines from *King Lear*, as it were, before a home audience expecting lines and actions from *The Music Man*.

Is Anyone Listening? Most of us have had a feeling that no one was listening to us. "I'm talking, but does anyone hear me?" We worry when we think it is important to communicate well with a special person or group and the communication becomes increasingly difficult.

Sometimes forthright communication with oneself becomes necessary. Many of my clients became quite frustrated because they had not learned to listen carefully to themselves. Or, to be more precise, individual clients seemed unable to explore certain critical subjects. Vagueness and distraction took over.

There are times when we do not want anyone to overhear us or to read our feelings. Jonathan could not talk forthrightly to himself about some of his feelings. He was convinced that it was unmanly to acknowledge them. Alicia complained that her husband had turned into a robot. "I married a wonderful man, but someone must have abducted him and replaced him with a look-alike that has no emotion other than anger."

Pleasure and Displeasure. In this section, let's look at the two feelings that are so basic that we have them common with other species. They are pleasure and displeasure. The word *hedonism* comes from the Greek *hedone*, which means "pleasure." Some public speakers seem to take great pleasure in denouncing hedonism. To be fair to them, I should note that they view hedonism as a life of debauchery or reckless abandon heedless of all consequences. What I wish to present, by contrast, is the elementary fact that from childhood we are favorably predisposed toward what we believe are sources of pleasure and are repelled by what we believe are sources of displeasure. Fortunately, pain has served as a warning that some activities or deprivation can bring injury or death. The state of water deprivation for a prolonged period is felt as pain or thirst. Fortunately, quenching it not only brings relief from deprivation, but also gives us pleasure. Imagine entering a kingdom that gives you an abundance of water, food, shelter, and numerous other benefits. In this kingdom, you have a vast range of opportunities as well as good health for as long as you wish. The one thing you will be denied in this kingdom of wealth and abundance is *pleasure*. Everything you do, see, hear, or taste will be void of pleasure. In short, nothing brings you enjoyment because pleasure does not exist in this kingdom. Furthermore, the kingdom offers no hope for enjoyment. Even your dreams of a better life give you no pleasure. All relationships with other human beings and animals flow smoothly, with no conflicts or animosities. The relationships, however, offer no pleasure, no enjoyment.

Imagine you have two options. You can live in this kingdom that gives you all your heart's desires with the exception of pleasure. The second option is the life you have now with both its pleasure and pain. Which would you choose?

Some people appear to believe that openly acknowledging or seeking pleasure itself is unworthy of human beings. While experiencing pleasure from various sources, they seem nevertheless to believe that pleasure should be accompanied by shame and perhaps guilt. Most of us have rightly experienced shame or guilt because of pleasure received in unjustifiable outbursts of anger, acts of revenge, or other deeds that violate our moral standards. We do not, however, regard pleasure per se to be evil. Indeed, torture is evil because it reduces the victim's pleasure sharply and replaces it with intense pain and perhaps serious injury that will guarantee suffering for months or years to come.

In listening carefully to ourselves, we realize that we have often endured the displeasures of a boring or stressful job that we could eventually gain access to major sources of enjoyment and security. Some people settle for permanently boring or stressful job so that we could eventually gain access to major sources of enjoyment and security. Some people settle for permanently boring or stressful work, not because pain attracts them, but because they can find no better job. In therapy, they have the possibility of acknowledging their own feelings. "Yes, I am during a heavy load of displeasure. Yes, I do long to develop new paths leading to more happiness. Okay, I admit I've been afraid of change because it can bring the pain of uncertainty…. So, what do I do now?"

In listening to ourselves carefully, we can understand that fear of change and its anticipated pain or displeasure has crippled our ability to imagine better choices. By being unable to admit or even recognize our fear, we take refuge in a vagueness that prevents us from addressing our fear. Perhaps we fear a person on the job, or fear making a mistake and looking foolish. By not acknowledging the fear's power over us, we lose the ability to face it realistically. It becomes a vicious circle. We have the fear, but we feel ashamed of having it. So, we leave it in a cloud of vagueness that turns the specific fear into a floating ambivalence with accompanying anxiety.

The Unconscious and the Subconscious. In 1960 at a state mental hospital, Arthur walked incessantly. The volunteer counselor could talk with him only if they walked and talked at the same time.

"Why do you walk inside this place all day?" the counselor asked.

"I'm walking away my sins."

"Could we perhaps run for a while to make some time for sitting down to talk?" asked the counselor.

This angered Arthur. Later, the counselor learned that Arthur, age 50, became agitated and irritated only on the days his mother came to visit him from nearby. After learning more about what Arthur's situation outside the hospital had been, the counselor wondered if Arthur's "crazy behavior" had been his way of getting into the asylum and away from his irritating mother.

The word asylum can mean (1) an institution for the cure of the mentally ill, or (2) a place offering protection or safety. Was Arthur seeing protection from his mother for at least six days a week? Perhaps another choice might have been to move to another state several hundred miles away from her.

Arthur appeared to be working unconsciously on the odd plan that sins were debts that could somehow be paid off by walking incessantly. Often we can learn if our plans are flawed or even crazy by pressing them for their implications and conclusions. Sometimes we think we are working in the hope of solving one problem when we are more likely dealing with another problem at the unconscious level.

Psychologists and psychiatrists tend to speak of "the unconscious" as the aspect of our mind that is unavailable for direct conscious scrutiny. "The subconscious" is the aspect that is more available. It isn't our secret self. We drive our cars and do hundreds of other things subconsciously—without observing ourselves doing them. But if called upon to describe what we were doing, we could describe them to some extent without fuss or resistance. We cannot live every moment of our waking time in a state of intense consciousness. That would be burdensome, inefficient, and probably dangerous. Most of our work has to be done at the subconscious level. A truck driver would quickly become dysfunctional and a danger to others if, while driving, he began observing himself and describing aloud his moves. "I'm approaching a traffic light and my foot is now touching the brake—lightly at first. I'm looking at my rearview mirrors and I'm listening to he loud motor off to my right, and I'm wondering if it's another truck, bus, or what. Now I'm pressing my foot on the brake again. Ah, the red light is now orange. I'm taking my foot off the brake. My hands are gripping the steering wheel. I can see a jet above against the clouds. Don't have to worry about the jet. But the car ahead is moving fast now. It's a red car."

If you were sitting beside the truck driver, you would want to urge him to forget putting into words what he is doing and thinking. You want him to cease talking so that he can give his full attention to the driving. If we placed a microphone at the piano for our favorite pianist to describe each of her movements, she would be wise to concentrate on playing and not on talking about her playing. Talking can interfere with her playing. Later, she can talk with her teacher about her technique.

There are appropriate and useful times to talk about our behavior and feelings. Some of our activities, feelings, and thoughts seem to resist being talked about. We become uncomfortable or even angry if someone tries to put them into words. Just as we have to convince a child not to resist us when we try to remove a splinter from his finger, so a friend or therapist must sometimes convince us to talk about certain feelings, thoughts, or actions that have become disturbing psychological splinters that make us irritable, unhappy, or unable to function as we would like.

Talking about Pleasure and Pain. Since depressed individuals do not always understand why they are depressed, they have difficulty in countering it. According to the surgery model, therapy and counseling can help the client cut into his history to find the event that needs to be removed. The event is "there" causing pain and preventing the client from living a fulfilling life. Together the client and therapist locate the traumatic event and, by verbal skills and careful examination, can remove it.

This raises the question of how anyone can "remove" an event that has already happened, there is also the practical problem of knowing whether the "event" really happened. Or, assuming it did, is it the real *cause* of the depression?

Another model, which offers more promise, may be called the "adult perspective model." Hank Benton, at the age of ten, saw a movie that scared him so much that he remembered the fright for many years. At the age of forty-two, he chanced to see that the movie would be on TV. He decided to watch it in the hope of confronting his fear again. With anticipation, he watched every scene. At the end, he told his wife, "It's a mediocre movie, and it's a little silly." He could not understand why he had been so frightened by it. As an adult, he could only smile at it. He felt a little disappointed that it did not scare him as an adult.

Not all events that disturbed us in the past prove innocuous. Some are traumatic and need to be dealt with from the adult perspective. In many cases, the fallibility of memory makes an accurate reconstruction of the past event or events difficult, if not impossible. Therapy, then, does not come by remembering with perfect accuracy the reputed crucial event. Rather, therapy emerges during the desensitizing process of talking intelligently, openly, and courageously about the feelings, thoughts, beliefs, and other matters relevant to the reputed disturbing event.

As a child, Nora Austen knew that her father was an alcoholic whose money spent on alcohol deprived his family of food and decent housing. Her neighbors' criticisms of her father cut deeply. Years later, she looked at him from an adult's perspective and acknowledged that he was indeed an irresponsible father and that most of the criticism was justified. She learned to face the fact that she had been deprived of a good father-daughter relationship. Although acknowledging the source of her pain, she did not feed her anger or use her childhood misfortune as a reason to slip into depression.

Explicating the Adult Perspective. The adult approach to misfortune is to have the appropriate response, which is easier said than done. Grieving the loss of someone dear takes time. A friend can help, since talking about the loss, the pain, and other relevant matters is the process of turning some of the unconscious and the subconscious into the conscious. After the misfortune, the memories and their emotions may continue for many years. We need to deal with them at the conscious level. Expectations continue, too. Are they realistic? If not, we need to revise them. At the unconscious level, we might have been living by expectations that did not have a chance of fulfillment. At the unconscious level, we might have been attempting to guide our lives by unrealistic plans and goals. Once we become conscious of them, we can become more specific in revising or replacing them.

Becoming Specific. Consciousness is a way of being specific about our lives. Unconsciousness leaves things in a stream of vagueness, letting matters take care of themselves. Much of life is carried on this way. There is much to say for the smoothness of routine. We do not want to stop and focus on every detail.

We need to stop and think consciously when big problems surface or when we anticipate a major problem. If the routine isn't flowing, it might be time to examine it. Can we locate the problem *specifically*?

Janice went to a counselor to say her marriage was "going downhill."

"Can you be specific?"

"It's just not what I want in a marriage. Hank isn't happy either."

For several minutes, Janice spoke in generalities. "Our marriage has gone sour." "He doesn't really love me." "I don't feel the same about him."

Gradually, her counselor guided her to talk about specifics. When we enter our doctor's office, we expect her to be specific. We would not expect the doctor to say, "Well, my diagnosis is: You are ill."

Karl knew he needed help. He went to a therapist and said, "Something has to be done about my depression. I've been in this slump for three months and I'm not getting any better."

The therapist would not let him generalize. Karl had said, "Life sucks."

"No, Karl. *Your* life sucks for the present. Let's find out why. When was your last physical exam?"

Eventually, the therapist and Karl learned that he was filled with resentment. Karl then wanted to say he was resentful of life in general. This generalization changed to the claim that those he worked with at the office no longer respected him.

"What is it about you that they no longer respect?"

"Me! They don't respect *me*! I'm just there—like a fly on the wall."

Together, the therapist and Karl kept problem for specifics. Yes, those at the office no longer included him in their conversations. They had their own world.

Eventually, Karl came to see that he could not expect to become a part of the new "in group" at work. He deeply resented being no longer the man they called upon to deal with certain problems they could not solve. "Karl, you can remain resentful for the rest of your life, but it won't change your situation at work," said the therapist.

"I'm just supposed to let them treat me like an outcast?"

"Do they direct insulting remarks at you?"

"No. They don't make any comments at all. Jus the minimal communication to get the work done."

After three sessions, Karl and his therapist worked on a twofold plan. First, Karl was to focus on one person on the job who might relate to him in a pleasant way. That person was Bart, a father of two children. Second, Karl was to focus on his recent discovery that Wayne, a fellow in a nearby office, seemed reasonably pleasant and interesting. Eventually, Wayne and Karl discovered they had common interests. They also invited Bart to lunch. Occasionally, Wayne's friend Heather joined them. Karl's depression faded primarily because he had new friends who were interesting. His therapist helped him see that he had no right to be resentful of the men who had not included him in their circle. "After all, Karl, you don't include everyone in your new circle, do you?" in time, Karl had to face reality about himself. He had resented the fact that he *needed* friends. The therapist helped him see that he had developed this odd resentment and generalization because he had felt rejected by those he worked with at the office.

"Karl, they had a right not to want you as their friend. They were not saying you are dirt. They simply preferred each other. You don't need to change them, do you?"

"So, you're saying I should enjoy the friends I have and let go of my resentment?"

"That's what you're saying, Karl, and I couldn't have said it better."

Sometimes, the agony of grief comes with anger and humor. Friends and therapists can help us acknowledge our mixed feelings. Feelings are specific and can change over the years because of their dependency on specific beliefs and expectations that change. In becoming adults, we revise the image of our parents, either moderately or radically; and thus our feelings about them modify.

The adult perspective includes very specific revisions in some of our expectations. What we believe about our friends and relatives is mostly the expectations we have of them. Some people change their religion by changing what they expected from it. Others change their expectations of political parties and personalities. Most of us "bargain with life" in the sense that we expect life to treat us in certain ways. Some versions of insanity are expectations that persist despite overwhelming falsification of the expectations. For twenty years, a mother in the Midwest expected to see her son return home from the war in Europe. He never returned. She continued to believe because she had turned her expectation into a moral duty. Confusing a mother's tenacious love with magical thinking, she felt that her ceasing to expect him to return home would actually kill him.

The bargains with life can leave us bitter and angry until we rethink the bargain and see it mostly our own insistence that "life" go according to our expectations. Somewhere along the way, we have to admit that the bargain was our own making. "Life" did not sign our agreement. We imposed it and then perhaps we became bitter because the imaginary "other" failed us. Bad things sometimes do happen to good people, just as good things can happen to bad people.

RESONATE

Resonate in Freedom. To resonate psychologically and socially is to enjoy fulfillment and harmony with oneself and others. To reach this level is a kind of well-coordinated freedom that has a "feel" of its own. I will merely touch on the difficult philosophical issue of free will vs. determinism. One philosopher at a St. Louis meeting said she was *determined* to believe in free will. Another said he was *forced* to accept free will. "I didn't have a choice. After hearing the arguments for free will, I was forced to accept them."

When we read our unfavorable x-rays, we don't say, "Although I can see that according to the x-ray my finger is broken, I freely choose to believe it isn't."

In the free will vs. determinism debate, it is useful to remember that we differ from other species in one profound way. Strong evidence and sound arguments can *compel* us to believe something even if we do not want to believe it. At the same time, if we are rational we *want to be compelled* be evidence and reason rather than by our whims even when the conclusion is not what we wanted. I would like to believe my finger is not broken, but only if in fact it isn't. Clearly, we frequently have conflicting wants or desires. The desire for the truth about our finger's damaged condition conflicts with our desire that the finger not be damaged.

An individual's daily life usually has several situations in which two perfectly sane and healthy desires come into conflict. We have learned that desiring the truth about even painful reality has served us well over the centuries even though the truth compels us to acknowledge the existence of undesirable facts.

Some people will pray for a certain desirable state of affairs in the future to become real, and they will pray for an undesirable state to not come about. When an event has already happened in the past, however, they will not seriously pray that it did not happen. They *wish* or *hope* that it hadn't happened. They do not believe that even God could literally unmake what has already taken place. For a reason, those who pray do not want all the prayers of everyone in the world to be answered. Such a world would be literally no world at all. The laws and patterns of nature would be suspended. If they had to choose between their living in a world in which *all* prayers were answered or *none*, which would they choose?

Freedom and Reality. Freedom is satisfaction of our wants or desires. In the real world, one-hundred percent freedom is a fiction because no one can satisfy all his or her desires. The physical world both satisfies some desires and prevents others from gaining satisfaction. Parents, friends, teachers, electricians, plumbers, and others pass on to us the fruit of their experiences in dealing with the *physical* environment. The *social* environment, likewise, affords means both to advance our freedom and to curtail it severely. Since we need to live with others, we have to come to terms with *their* wants either through cooperation, conflict, or a policy of live-and-let-live. The social institutions both help us gain freedom and restrain us. Ideally, the institutions arrest some of our desires so that better ones can flourish. Traffic laws are a clear example. Stop signs, traffic lights, and speed limits are only a few of the constraints on our freedom. On the other hand, without them, the traffic would approach chaos. The rational rules that limit us make possible our freedom to drive. We suppress some desires so that the weaker and better ones may have a chance.

At the *individual* level, restraint or suppression of some desires is an inescapable fact. This is the psychological reality with no exceptions! Each person is forced to choose the desires to develop and the ones to suppress or eliminate. Bill wants to be a happily married man. Unfortunately, he does not know how to relate sensitively and intelligently to a woman that could contribute to his happiness. He lacks certain personal skills. He is not free to participate in a happy marriage until he changes some of his behavior and extinguishes or sublimates some of his desires. Ironically, he might consider the advantages of *wanting* to change some of what he wants. Self-discipline is basically the process of cutting off or reducing the satisfaction of some desires to satisfy certain others. There is no freedom per se. There is freedom *from* this or that specifically, and freedom *to* do or have this or that specifically.

Freedom and Reason. The job of reason is to help sort out what we really want from what we just want. A great deal of reasoning goes into tracking our desires to see how they network and strengthen each other or how they conflict. If you are in the business of marketing swimsuits for women, you can *desire* to grow rich by marketing your product in Saudi Arabia. But you are not free to sell them there. You are free to *try* to make contact with a retailer in, say, Mecca. But *trying* is not *selling*. If your goal is to try, then continue. But your profit will be skimpier than your swimsuits.

In "The Clerk's Tale," Chaucer portrays Walter, Marquis of Saluzzo, as the highest born man in Lombardy. The people send a deputation urging him to marry. He is popular and they want to be sure his successor will be acceptable. Marriage is, however, far from Walter's mind, which is mostly on hunting, hawking, and jealousy guarding his brand of freedom, that is, doing what he wants today with little regard for the future or other people. He is detached and not someone who should be married. In the story, he agrees to marry a woman, provided she is "the gentlest" in the land. He will agree to his wedding only if she is at the bottom of the hierarchy. Chaucer describes the marriage in grim detail. It is virtually a clinical description of a pathological relationship. [Bernard J. Paris, *Imagined Human Beings: A Psychological Approach to Character and Conflict in Literature* New York: New York University Press, 1997.] (82-92). Chaucer's point may be that under the mere label "marriage," strange relationships can be observed. Walter could not have been happily married, however, because he lacked even the elementary qualities essential to friendship.

Want and Really Want. In examining and comparing our vast range of wants and desires, we can rank some of them in a hierarchy of preference. Much of the process of sorting and prioritizing proceeds at the unconscious and subconscious levels. The subconscious process can be trained to operate both more imaginatively and more critically. Whether at the conscious level or not, reasoning about our wants entails determining the ones we really want after we make the comparisons and evaluations.

It is imperative to understand that what we truly want or desire will often not be our strongest desire. In fact, some of our strongest desires are the very ones we strongly wish to eliminate. We really do not want them, for they will seriously interfere with our wider freedom. Because some strong desires can bring disaster, we reinforce the weaker ones that we strongly approve of. We seek encouragement from friends or from whomever or whatever will assist us in strengthening our preferred desires and weakening those that are strong but not acceptable.

A race car driver is free to pursue his goal only if he arrests and even starves some of his desires and impulses. Without that restraint, he could quickly lose his life. Artists, musicians, skier, chefs, boxers, surgeons—all must subdue many of their desires and impulses if they really want to pursue and perfect their basic passion. To eliminate all restraints is to wipe out every branch of freedom. To follow every impulse is to become an emotional wreck, a slave. Psychological anarchy is chaos and the demise of freedom. Uncontrolled freedom is the road to a psychological collision.

Addiction. From a psychological perspective, what is an addiction? It is a practice driven by a strong or overwhelming desire that is usually intensely satisfying. That is one side of the coin. On the other side, the satisfaction undermines many other satisfaction that have been crucial to the individual's life. Addiction functions as a parasite robbing the individual of a wide range of personal freedoms. In a Southern state, an exceptional high-school running back had enriched the lives of others and was opening new doors of opportunity for his future. The doors closed quickly when he exercised his freedom to experiment with drugs. Soon, the drugs took control, crippling his other freedoms. In time, he lost still more freedoms when he went to prison. One powerful single freedom (to enjoy drugs) wiped out a vast network of other freedoms. Because he did not arrest his desire to experiment with drugs, he lives most of his life now under arrest and confinement.

An addiction has two faces. The first is the "high," the extreme pleasure. The second face is not so pretty. The addict begins to feel irritated, ill at ease, and uncomfortable. Without the substance or whatever, the addict begins to suffer. He or she is not at peace without the "fix." The substance has made itself necessary. The addict has placed himself in a state of deprivation so intense that he feels he cannot go on without the fix. A new "hunger" has now become a part of his life. In many cases, he suffers utter agony until he feeds his new hunger. Some addicts will lie, steal, or even kill to gain temporary relief from the agony.

In Texas, the successful alcoholic Tim Karner took every opportunity to feed his craving for alcohol. Gradually, he increased his opportunities to drink. Tim Karner paid a heavy price to attain his goal of becoming a successful alcoholic. His wife filed for divorce, and his children lost respect for him. To be sure, he wanted their love and respect. Btu his craving for alcohol proved to be stronger and more persistent. He wanted to live longer and to excel as a teacher, but the freedom to consume alcohol under a variety of circumstances and upon a variety of occasions proved increasingly unrestrained and unyielding. Did he accomplish what he wanted? Like everyone else, he accomplished some of what he wanted. He certainly excelled in drinking heavily and often. Rarely did he permit anyone or anything to interfere with his aspect of his freedom. *He died a successful alcoholic.* As a man wanting respect and to be a loving member of the community, he proved a failure. Alcohol was supremely important to him. His wife and children were less important.

Most people learn to distinguish some of what they want from what they *really* want. This comes about by acknowledging that in one way or another, some cravings will have to be toned down or eliminated so that the better desires can gain special fortification. The noted American novelist, Janet Evanovich, recently confessed she craved abandoned birthday cakes, which she could purchase for half-off. She bought the cakes not merely to look at, but to eat while writing. This powerful, almost overwhelming, desire gave her intense pleasure—plus thirty unnecessary pounds. Because her readers want to continue reading her wonderful novels for years to come, they hope she will severely curtail her habit of eating cakes.

The Person as a Unified Force for Value. Much of what we call counseling provided by friends and professionals involves helping us develop a life style that brings the more constructive desires together into a coordinated force resembling a well-rehearsed orchestra. Fortunately, our brain has a neocortex that encourages long-term commitment, which includes the maternal and family affection that reptiles lack. Instead of cannibalizing our young, we protect them. From the initial bonding, we learn other commitments and long-term planning that allows us to coordinate our better desires into an astonishing creative force. Thanks to our neocortex, we can create an entire system of self-reinforcement. It is as if each of us is a community of instruments that can be attuned to one another. [Daniel Goleman, Emotional Intelligence: Why It Can Matter More than IQ (New York: Bantam Books, 1995.] (11)

Responsible for Our Own Arrangement. We not only can be like many instruments playing in harmony, but can also follow our own creative arrangement. We become a perpetual production that can take the good fortune that comes our way and crate a dynamic character developing into an ethical personality. This includes the willingness to sacrifice and work for long-run goals and values. Each of us can be moved by what is not before our eyes or in our immediate range. A vision of a better self can move us into the present so that we not only benefit from our social environment and our culture, but also contribute to them, thus making our lives more meaningful.

Conversing With a Recorder. Most of what we value involves relating to other people. Imagine you are the only human being alive on the planet. You have a recorder with a limitless supply of batteries.

You have also a dog (Jupie) and a supply of canned goods to feed both of you for many years. Which one would you spend more time with—the recorder or Jupie? With the recorder, you can exchange ideas with yourself and then listen to yourself day after day. You will perhaps learn a lot about yourself. But you know that upon your death, no one will ever hear your recorded words. You are your sole audience.

You want, of course, to talk to Jupie because she will respond to your voice and your actions. You can develop a friendship with her but not with the tape recorder. Eventually, you realize that although Jupie can hear your voice and respond to it, she can *understand* very little of what you are saying. No matter how intelligent, she will understand only a small portion of what you say.

Clearly, we talk to be understood. Furthermore, we want to hear and understand another person. In our dreams, we create other persons. Soliloquies are rare in the dream world. Imagine you live in a community in which no one, including your spouse, disagrees with you—ever. In ordinary conversation, we want to encounter another mind with ideas and beliefs different from our own.

"When two people agree on everything, one of them is unnecessary." Ruth Graham

To genuinely disagree with another person, you must first understand her. When serving on committees or at work, you need disagreements. Ironically, disagreeableness reduces the probabilities of honest disagreement. Honest disagreement in a context of mutual regard increases the probability of gaining more understanding and insight.

Friendship is interesting because of shared interests and enjoyable challenges. So, we care for friendship—literally *take care* to respect and cultivate it. This includes paying attention, listening, and comprehending. Active listening is more than serving as a recorder of words. To listen actively is an art of comprehending and responding. It is *not* mind reading. It *is* taking time to share thoughts, feelings, meanings, and suggestions. We try to shoot down some of our theories in order to improve them or replace them with better ones. We do not shoot down our friends in order to reform or replace them. Yet, in friendship, criticism might be required on appropriate occasions. Friendship is not a science; it is an art to be practiced sensitively. Sometimes, criticism of a friend's theory, plan, or behavior might be required of friendship. Necessary criticism can be offered in a context of friendship and good will. We all know personally that if we are not put on the defense, we learn more readily. Since everyone needs to have his expectations and plans looked at with an honest critical eye, we do well to accept solid criticism as a gift to be put to good use. Perhaps the best expression of gratitude is the wise use of the good criticism and helpful counsel.

Breinigsville, PA USA
24 March 2011
258399BV00002B/9/P

9 781451 274974